THE ENGLISH LAKE DISTRICT

In Pictures

HEAD OF BUTTERMERE AND HIGH CRAG

BUTTERMERE, with the neighbouring lakes of Crummock and Loweswater, is in the charge of the National Trust. Although small—just over a mile long and less than a half wide—it yet gives an impression of real grandeur. High Crag, its flanks scarred by winter torrents, rises to 2,443 feet; a path to Ennerdale and Wasdale leads over the shoulder to its left.

THE ENGLISH LAKE DISTRICT

In Pictures

FOREWORD AND INTRODUCTIONS BY
THE RT. HON. SIR NORMAN BIRKETT, P.C.
PAST PRESIDENT, FRIENDS OF THE LAKE DISTRICT

ILLUSTRATIONS DESCRIBED BY PHILIP CLEAVE
SECRETARY, FRIENDS OF THE LAKE DISTRICT

CONTENTS

*

ODHAMS PRESS LTD. LONG ACRE, LONDON

RIVER DERWENT, BORROWDALE

FAMED for its salmon and trout, the Derwent sweeps over a rocky bed between splendid woods of oak and beech, with a profusion of silvery birches. Just below the spot pictured, at the Jaws of Borrowdale, the poet Gray, on his famous journey in 1769, turned back daunted by the frowning precipices which guard the entrance to the dale. Thus he missed seeing what, in the opinion of many experienced travellers, is the finest valley in England.

Foreword

THIS book was designed to give pleasure to all sorts and conditions of men and women whatever their knowledge of the Lake District might be. There are some who know that lovely spot, the loveliest in all England to my way of thinking, just as they know the features and expression of somebody they love. They know the hills and mountains by their lovely names; they can tell you not only the names, but the situation of every lake; they know the mountain passes, the old tracks across the hills and the footpaths; the quiet, remote, unfrequented gem-like tarns; the rivers that run to the sea, and the little becks that fill them as they sing through the lonely dales; and the one-inch map of the district is like the score of a much-loved musical composition, known by heart and capable of being read at sight to recall every familiar feature.

And there are some who fall short of this standard of perfection. They are the majority who know many of the mountains and lakes, many of the tracks across the fells, some solitary and secluded places they have discovered for themselves, a few delightful inns and farmhouses and villages, and a few very favourite spots to which they continually return. They are not quite so well versed in all that makes the Lake District, but they love it with an enduring love. And no doubt there are some, as Professor Housman said of himself when recalling at Cambridge the sight of Wordsworth drunk and Porson sober, who stand "Betwixt and Between." There is yet another class who, surprisingly enough, do not know the Lake District at all, or who have merely passed through it on the high road to some other and less favoured destination.

I had the good fortune to be born on the very fringe of the Lake District, some nine miles from the foot of Lake Windermere. In one day's excursion one could go through the Norse village of Greenodd to Newby Bridge and Lakeside, sail up Lake Windermere to Ambleside, reach Dungeon Gill and climb the Langdale Pikes, scramble over the fells past the incredibly beautiful Codale Tarn, and passing Easedale Tarn descend into Grasmere, take a coach drawn by four horses to Ambleside, sail down the lake, and so home. A boyhood and youth filled with days of this kind has made me a kind of Lakeland evangelist, and I must have heard very many times: "But it always rains there," or the variant on the old countryman's saying: "There's nowt here but scenery."

This book, I therefore repeat, is for everybody, just as Lakeland is for everybody, too, from the youngest to the oldest. Its purpose is to try and capture in pictures some of the surpassing beauty of the Lake District. The Lake District, of course, belongs to three counties—Cumberland, Westmorland, and Lancashire —but to those who know and love that delectable spot county boundaries mean nothing at all. The Lake District is one and indivisible. The passing of the National Parks and Access to the Countryside Act of 1949 has set the seal upon this view, for the Lake District is to be one of the first National Parks with all the most beautiful parts of each county gathered into the one whole. That achievement, the result of long years of devoted labour, gives hope of better methods of preservation as well as for larger means of enjoyment; and it is entirely fitting therefore that a book of this nature, designed for all, should appear at this time, when more and more people may be expected to come to the National Park.

Pictures can bring to the mind and to the imagination something that the most eloquent and moving prose might fail to do. For whatever grace of words a man may have (and the Lake District has never failed for descriptive writers), it is impossible that he should be able to set down on the printed page in a few words the unique beauty of this corner of England in its amplitude. Turn the pages of this book to the two famous views familiar to thousands the world over, the sight of the Vale of Newlands from Catbells, or the sight of Rydal Water (Reedy Rydal) from Loughrigg Fell. Think of them in all the glory of early summer. The sky, the clouds, the trees, the fields, the gurgling becks that "tumble as they run," the still waters and the encompassing hills—all combine in some quite mysterious way to fill the mind and the heart with a sense of wonder and glory for which the ordinary man can find no adequate expression. A Wordsworth with the immortal gift of the "inward eye" and the power to give immortal expression to the thing seen can speak for all men; but ordinary folk can but "stand and stare."

Therefore, this book seeks to re-create in the mind the natural beauty of the Lake District in its infinite variety and to do it by means of beautiful photographs. It was the great Bacon who observed in the *Essays* that "a man can scarce allege his own merits with modesty, much less extol them"; and as I have had nothing whatever to do with the photographs in this book, I might perhaps be allowed to say that they seem to me to catch and portray the authentic atmosphere of Lakeland for all those who have eyes to see.

Without attempting to analyse the indescribable charm of the Lake District, perhaps one or two rather obvious comments may be made within the proper limits of a Foreword. The first is to note how small the district is, and how infinite are the riches contained in the little room. It has been said with truth that a man may walk across it in a good day's walking, for it is but thirty miles or thereabouts across. From Skiddaw and Blencathra to the foot of Windermere, and from Ennerdale to Haweswater, lie the rough limits. It is almost unbelievable that within this small area lie 180 mountains and 65 lakes and tarns. Most of the

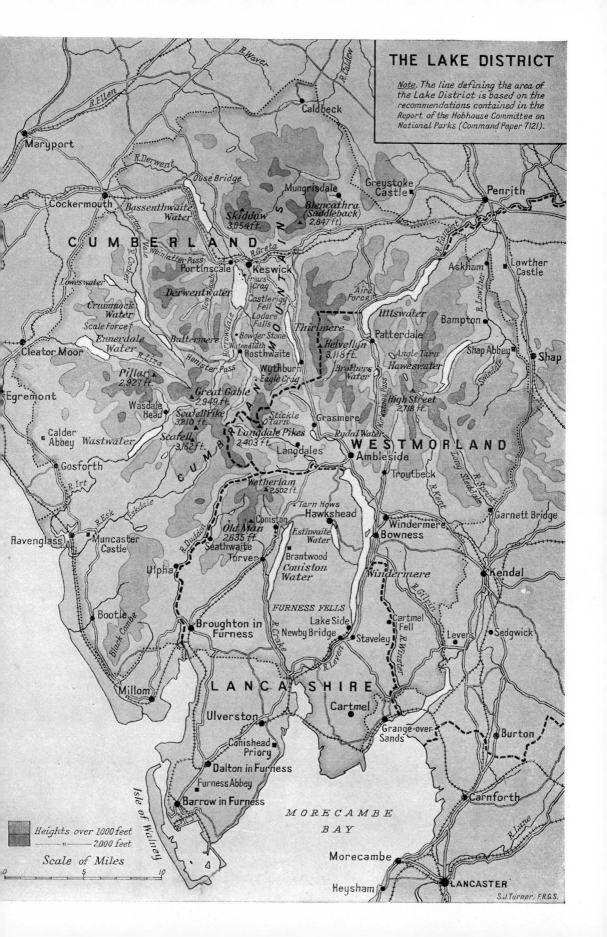

AIRA FORCE

A SLENDER fall more than 60 feet high in a dell of romantic charm, Aira Force figures in
Wordsworth's tragic poem, "The Somnambulist"—a legend about a sleep-walking maiden
who, surprised at midnight on the bridge, falls fatally into the chasm. The waterfall and
the surrounding 750 acres of Gowbarrow Park are held by the National Trust. From the
hillsides of the Park are gained striking views of all three reaches of Ullswater.

mountains are over 2,000 feet in height, some of them reaching 3,000 feet, but rising as they do from the dale heads they can yet convey an overwhelming sense of grandeur. Those who have seen the magnificence of the Canadian Rockies or the solemn splendours of the Swiss mountains can still find in the Lake District something not to be found elsewhere. Those who know the Canadian lakes can still find in Grasmere and Rydal and Crummock and Loweswater a great joy in their very smallness.

The history of these hills and lakes and mountain passes is a fascinating story as told by the geologists and the historians. To those who know this story even in its simplest form the enjoyment of the beauty of Lakeland is much enhanced. It has never been better told than by that great Lakeland figure, the Rev. H. H. Symonds, in his little classic, *Walking in the Lake District*. And beautifully does he point the moral. "And so some faint awareness, never more, of how the hills came to stand in their present order; of the qualities of certain plants which grow in high cold places; of the history caught in local names; of the races of men which have built the traditions of a district, and shaped its ways of feeling; all this adds a zest, an intelligence, a scope to walking, and makes an art of it, an orchestration of many powers and interests." Through millions of years the processes of nature have formed the marvellous outlines of the hills, the great rocks, the wonderful vegetation, the great stretches of water and all that we look on today. If, when at Keswick, you climb any of the surrounding hills and look towards Skiddaw and compare that sight with the sight of Great End or the Scafell Pikes, the difference of form and view speaks of great movements in widely separated ages.

It is this variety of outline that continues to lend enchantment, and holidays in the Lake District can be renewed again and again because of the particular charm which belongs to particular places. A holiday at Grasmere can be quite a different thing from a holiday at Ennerdale. Grasmere is the very heart of the Lake Country. It is a vale of quietness set in encircling hills. Its lake, as you come to it from Red Bank, is a sight never to be forgotten. And there is something added, for as Professor Trevelyan has said: "Places like books have an interest or a beauty of association, as well as an absolute or aesthetic beauty." Grasmere has for ever linked its name and its beauty with the great name of Wordsworth. These are the hills over which he walked, this is the scene on which he once brooded, and here it is that he now lies at rest in the quiet churchyard. Here at Dove Cottage his mighty genius reached its height, and a holiday at Grasmere is enriched by the memories of the man who could write for us:

> Love had he found in huts where poor men lie;
> His daily teachers had been woods and rills,
> The silence that is in the starry sky,
> The Sleep that is among the lonely hills.

But Ennerdale has a solitary air about it, sometimes even a deserted air, and it is perhaps the least visited of all the lakes. But come to it from Carlisle or Workington and the first sight of Ennerdale Water with the grey hills about it is one of rare solemnity and beauty. And seated in the charming and comfortable little Angler's Inn (as I still prefer to call it, though "hotel" has got on to the notepaper) you can hear the lake water lapping with low sounds by the front windows, and looking out see one of the most famous skylines in the whole of Lakeland, with the famous Pillar, Scoatfell and Steeple, and feel that the world with all its cares is very far away.

But in reflecting on the geologists' wonderful story it is well to remember that much of the beauty we prize in Lakeland is man-made. The charm and character of many of the dale heads is due to the fact that they have been continuously farmed for many generations. "Few scenes in England," said Anthony Collett in *The Changing Face of England*, "are either what Nature first made them or the product of the single purpose of man. They bear the stamp of two or three thousand years of almost continual modelling; the architecture of the fields and hills is of as many periods as that of the churches they embosom."

The attraction of Lakeland is not confined to the rugged mountains or the placid shining lakes or to the great mountain passes or the glory of the fells and becks. It lies also in the cultivated fields, in the grasslands, in the Herdwick sheep roaming the hillsides, in the peaceful dales which run into the heart of the mountains, in the little whitewashed cottages scattered everywhere throughout the district, in the diminutive and historic churches, in the amazingly beautiful stone bridges which cross the rivers, in the attractive wayside inns, in the irregular stone walls that run crazily along the hillsides, in the wealth of oak and birch and rowan and yew and ash, and in the wild and wayward hedges.

Here then are photographs of this great mountain sanctuary, this great playground, this land of delight. To the young it can be very heaven. Rock-climbing of the most adventurous kind, walking of unequalled character, fishing, rowing, sailing, camping, nature-study—all made more delightful by the hospitality and kindness of the local people. To those whose days of full activity are past, the Lake District offers gentle walks in the midst of the most perfect scenery on which the eye can look, mountain and sea air, and a contemplative quietude that restores both body and mind. And perhaps the greatest boon that this book can bestow is to bring to those in great cities these great pictures of natural beauty, when perhaps they are unable to go and see them, and when the mind hungers for the sight of them. It is not yet sufficiently realized how great is the need for the sight of natural beauty nor what blessings can come from its satisfaction.

NORMAN BIRKETT

A GLIMPSE OF BOWFELL

BOWFELL, the most graceful of mountains, gives the impression, especially when under snow, of being very much loftier than its actual height of 2,960 feet. From its narrow, tapering summit striking views are obtained—to Windermere in the east, whilst in the west, across the gulf of Eskdale, the Scafell group rises majestically. In this view, from above Skelwith Bridge, the pastoral foreground contrasts finely with the snow-capped peak.

HONISTER PASS: THE WAY TO BUTTERMERE

HONISTER CRAG, more than 2,000 feet high, overlooks the pass leading from Borrowdale to Buttermere. For above two hundred years roofing slate of the finest quality has been quarried at Honister, the slate being taken from galleries deep inside the crag. The tramway in the right foreground is part of the workings on Yew Crag, which confronts Honister Crag.

The North

THIS rough division of the Lake District into North, South, East, and West is done for the convenience of the reader and for no other purpose. There is no essential difference between any of the areas, and indeed they merge into each other in the most attractive way. Mr. Cleave has appended such concise and admirable descriptive notes to the photographs that the characteristic features of each district receive their proper emphasis, and do not require further elaboration in a book which is essentially a picture book. But a short word of introduction to each section may not be out of place, for they each have something peculiar to themselves whilst sharing the same elemental things.

The northern district, for example, can claim in some senses to be the oldest part of the Lake District, for the area which includes Cockermouth and Keswick is made of the rocks we know as "Skiddaw Slates" because they are to be seen in Skiddaw itself. These Skiddaw Slates are said by the geologists to be at least 500 million years old; and underneath them lie rocks that are very much older still. I mentioned in the Foreword the connexion between geological formation and the form of the scenery; and in this northern area the scenery is of the grandest possible description.

Among the mountains, Skiddaw and Saddleback stand supreme; Saddleback being perhaps better known by its older and lovelier name of Blencathra. It seems to accord with the general fitness of things that Skiddaw should have been one of the first mountains to be climbed, not as some extraordinary feat, but simply for the sake of the wonderful views to be obtained from the summit. Towards the end of the seventeenth century the views from the top of Skiddaw were certainly very well known and were the subject of much remarkable writing. Skiddaw is described as "this stupendous mountain," and the most terrifying accounts are given of its chasms, and ravines, and precipitous rocks. Gentle old ladies in sandshoes wander up Skiddaw today in comparative ease and enjoy much the same prospect as the early climbers. But Blencathra is a much more satisfying mountain to climb. When John Ruskin made his first climb there he thought it the finest thing he had seen up to that time in the whole district.

The chief lakes are Derwentwater and Bassenthwaite. Bassenthwaite has a quiet charm of its own, but Derwentwater has some claim to be regarded as the most beautiful lake in the whole of the Lake District. The photographs in this book would seem to lend strong support for that contention. The view from

Friar's Crag was thought by Ruskin to be among the very finest in the whole of Europe. It is easily reached from Keswick and now commemorates Ruskin and that other great friend and defender of natural beauty, Canon H. D. Rawnsley, who followed Wordsworth in defending the Lake District from attack from any quarter. Keswick is the most popular centre for the whole of this district, though it is a little too populous at times for the tastes of those who love solitude and seclusion. It lies on the main road that leads to Grasmere, and Ambleside, and the South, and the modern motor-coaches bring hundreds of visitors in the season from all the Lancashire towns. Men and women from all over the world have made Keswick their centre, and some have made it their home. Among the great ones of the earth, Shelley came here for his honeymoon; Coleridge, Southey, De Quincey, Charles Lamb and Ruskin knew it well; and the whole neighbourhood will always have a kind of immortality in the pages of English literature.

The other possession of this district which must be mentioned is the famous and lovely vale of Borrowdale. There are some who call it the loveliest vale in all England, and if you turn to the remarkable photograph of it in this book you may be of the same opinion. In Borrowdale there is almost everything that Lakeland has to offer—great undulating fells, wonderful rocky crags, woods and fields, waterfalls and singing becks, the majesty of the mountains, the beauty of Derwentwater, and some of the most characteristic and attractive villages, like Rosthwaite and Seatoller, Stonethwaite and Seathwaite. The photographs in this book will recall to many the days when from Seatoller they climbed some of the great mountains, refreshed themselves at the little tarns or the wandering becks, took in the glory of the distant views, and came down from the heights in the evening to some lonely farmhouse or quiet inn beautifully and deliciously tired to reflect upon all the glories of the long day.

It is scarcely necessary to add that the mood of peace and satisfaction which then descends like a benediction is only given to those who walk. Leslie Stephen said that on such occasions he fancied himself a felicitous blend of poet and saint; but the plain truth remains that for those who would see any part of the Lake District as it ought to be seen, so that it will yield up its most precious secrets, the golden rule is that they must walk. There are some who prefer to walk alone. They love the undisturbed and healing solitude. There are some who delight in walking parties with all the laughter and chatter of bright companions. There can be no rule in these things; they depend on individual taste. For myself, give me the companion of my own choosing, who loves the open road as I do, in whose company I can be happy whatever befall, who can be silent for miles, and then illumine the day with some lovely remembered line the scene evokes, and I ask no more of human felicity. And I must add in all thankfulness that all this has been vouchsafed unto me.

MUNGRISDALE CHURCH

THE little church at Mungrisdale is typical of the dales churches, simple and solid—"built first and architected after," as the local phrase has it. The dedication is to the Scottish saint, St. Kentigern (also known as St. Mungo), hence the village's name. The village is a good centre for exploring the wild country "back o' Skidda'" over which John Peel often hunted.

SKIDDAW AND DERWENTWATER FROM THE "LOOKOUT"

DERWENTWATER: TWO FAVOURITE VIEWPOINTS

THE view on the left is taken from farther north, and at a lower level, than that on the previous page. What is lost in extent is gained in charm and intimacy. The quiet road from Watendlath here crosses Ashness Bridge, typical of local craftsmanship in its unpretentious solidity. Skiddaw (3,054 feet) is easily recognized in the background. Ruskin said that the first thing he remembered as an event in his life was being taken to Friars Crag (*seen above*). The view from it, he claimed, is one of the five finest in Europe. The great man is commemorated by a slab of rough-hewn Borrowdale stone, with a simple inscription, which stands among the storm-tossed Scots firs crowning the rock. Both Friars Crag and Stable Hills, the farm seen here, are National Trust properties.

KESWICK—HUB OF LAKELAND

THE summer visitor does not see the Lake District in all its attractive aspects. Severe winters are unusual, but when the tarns and, more rarely, the lakes freeze over there is splendid sport. There is, surprisingly enough, a flourishing Ski Club; the best runs being on the long slopes north and east of Helvellyn. Crosthwaite, the parish church of Keswick, seen below, was founded by St. Kentigern, it is said in the year 553. The present building dates from the middle of the sixteenth century. Robert Southey, Poet Laureate 1813-43, worshipped here for forty years. His grave is in the churchyard; his effigy, with an epitaph by Wordsworth, in the church. Keswick's market charter dates from the time of Edward I. One of the town's principal streets is shown below, left. In the background, beyond Fitz Park, is well-wooded Latrigg (1,203 feet), an outlier of Skiddaw.

THE RIDGE OF CATBELLS

OF ALL the joys which the mountains offer, ridge-walking is probably the keenest. From Dale Head northwards to Catbells there is a high-level walk of over four miles, much of it on turf as smooth and soft as a bowling green. Below one's left hand lies the Vale of Newlands, a line of fine crags plunging headlong into it; on the right, first Borrowdale and then Derwentwater unfold their varied beauties. This picture, taken from Maiden Moor (1,887 feet), looks northwards to the summit of Catbells (1,482 feet). In the foreground the old corpse path from Borrowdale over to Newlands can be seen crossing a depression in the ridge. Skiddaw fills the horizon, with Keswick lying at its feet. Westwards from the town the rich flats of the Vale of Keswick lead the eye towards Bassenthwaite Water, the head of which can just be picked out. (Both Catbells and Maiden Moor are well shown in the view at the top of page 20; the latter peering over the two conical summits of the former.)

22

CASTLERIGG STONE CIRCLE

VERY impressive is the situation of the so-called Druids' Circle, really a Bronze Age relic long ante-dating any Druids. Although barely a mile away, Keswick is out of sight. So, too, are the softer beauties of the Derwentwater countryside. Except for the farmsteads scattered on the slopes of Blencathra, the scene is one of utter solitude; the silent hills standing round in sombre grandeur. There are thirty-eight stones, grouped in a circle whose perfect regularity is apparent when one looks down from the hills above, and a small inner group of ten stones more. A line drawn through the centre of the circle, pointing north-east to Fiends' Fell in the Pennines, passes through the great circle near Penrith called Long Meg and her Daughters: the direction of sunrise on May the First! The stones are now cared for by the National Trust. On the north there frowns the craggy front of Blencathra. The ascent is not hard, and from the summit (2,847 feet) the view of Thirlmere, and of Derwentwater and the surrounding mountains, is superb.

CONTRASTS NEAR KESWICK

Above, the fine old bridge which crosses the Derwent at Portinscale, a mile west of Keswick. Skiddaw forms a noble background. Below, Sharp Edge, Blencathra. The crossing of this ridge is no expedition for a windy day, but in normal conditions it is not difficult for anyone with a steady head. Straight below the Edge lies the dark Scales Tarn, so deep sunk that, according to the legend, at high noontide the stars may be seen reflected in its depths.

NEWLANDS CHURCH

THE neat, whitewashed structure is very small, for the entire congregation is drawn from a mere score of farms. The leafless winter scene is transformed in spring, when birch and beech show the tenderest green, and the churchyard is a mass of wild primroses and daffodils. The name of the valley refers to the land reclaimed by a drainage scheme in its lower reach. The Vale of Newlands, well displayed on pages 26-7, is surrounded by steep hills. Those seen are (*left to right*) Hindscarth (2,385 feet), Robinson (2,417 feet), and, farther off, Red Pike (2,479 feet). Buttermere lies between the last-named hill and the other two.

THE VALE OF NEWLANDS FROM CATBELLS

"D'YE KEN JOHN PEEL?"

JOHN PEEL—next to Wordsworth the most famous of Cumberland men—was born and buried at Caldbeck. Most of his life was spent at Greenrigg Farm, Ruthwaite (*seen left, above*). The well-known verses were written by John Woodcock Graves, a weaver and a friend of Peel's, and set to the old air called "Bonnie Annie." In Caldbeck churchyard (*left, below*) is Peel's grave, the stone decorated with hunting gear. The trees show an unusual variety: silver birches and both English and Irish yews. The massive strength of the tower is typical of the border churches. The Blencathra Foxhounds (*above*) are, in all but the literal sense, the descendants of Peel's own pack. Only during the hunting season are hounds kennelled together; through the summer they are boarded out with neighbouring farmers. The hunting is all on foot, for riding over the steep and rough fells is impossible.

THE HERRIES COUNTRY

WATENDLATH TARN (*seen above*) is a good example of these little upland meres, lying cupped in the lower hills, over which peer the great mountains. The finely-shaped peak is Great Gable, with Lingmell and Scafell Pike farther to the left. Crossing the hill beside the larch plantation can be seen the path leading to Rosthwaite, the nearest village. Hugh Walpole laid the scenes of his romantic "Herries" novels in the country round about Borrowdale and Keswick. He chose Watendlath as the home of Judith Paris. Rarely can fiction have been accepted more readily as fact; in one of the farms a "Judith Paris' staircase" (*left*) is shown. The flagged kitchen floor and stone stairs are typical.

30

"BACK O' SKIDDA'"

HALF a mile below the old packhorse bridge at Watendlath (*seen above*) is the "Churn," or Devil's Punchbowl, where the force of the water has scooped out a circular basin, from which it escapes by an invisible hole in the bottom. "Back o' Skidda'" is a wild region of sweeping moorlands—bents and heather and grouse—where one may wander for a day and never meet a soul. Skiddaw House (*right*)—"the loneliest house in England"—is the only habitation in the parish, and for many years the tenant was the sole voter on the list and had to be both clerk and chairman at all meetings. It figures largely in *The Fortress* by Hugh Walpole, who is here seen standing near-by in contemplative mood.

31

EAGLE CRAG, BORROWDALE

As IS well shown in the view on pages 34-5, Borrowdale branches into several subsidiary dales. Here the Langstrath Beck meets the rushing Greenup Gill, and forms the Stonethwaite Beck, which joins the Derwent in a couple of miles. Eagle Crag divides the two valleys, Greenup being on its left and Langstrath (out of sight) on its right.

THE HEART OF BORROWDALE

AGAIN we are looking into the Stonethwaite branch, towards Eagle Crag. The level strath, rich from constant alluvial deposits, provides the indispensable winter pasture for the hardy sheep which range in summer over the high fells. Quite striking is the unhappy effect created by a single house which, instead of having the native gable-end, is of the "villa" type.

BORROWDALE—ENGLAND'S GRANDEST VALLEY

Left to right, GLARAMARA (2,560 feet), GREAT END (2,984), SCAFELL PIKE
(3,210), SCAFELL (3,162), LINGMELL (2,649), and GREAT GABLE (2,949)

GRANGE IN BORROWDALE

BECAUSE an island divides the stream into two channels, the bridge at Grange (*seen above*) is a double one. The Derwent, flowing out of Borrowdale, enters Derwentwater about a mile below this point. The name Grange recalls the time when Borrowdale belonged to the Furness Abbey estates, and here was the grange, or barn where the monks stored their crops. The Bowder Stone (*left*) is an enormous boulder which stands, perfectly balanced, like a stranded ship resting on its keel. It measures 60 feet long and 35 feet high; its weight has been variously estimated but is probably about 2,000 tons. So narrow is the "keel" that two people can shake hands through a hole in its base.

36

COCKERMOUTH

BUILT soon after the Conquest, twice almost destroyed, burned by the Scots, and neglected after the Civil War, Cockermouth Castle (*right*) still stands four-square above the Derwent. A portion, indeed, is still habitable. Edmund Crouchback (brother of Edward I), Piers Gaveston, and Mary, Queen of Scots, all played a part in its history. As a boy, Wordsworth scrambled about among the ruins. In April, 1770, in a plain Georgian house in Main Street, Cockermouth, was born William Wordsworth, son of John Wordsworth, the Earl of Lonsdale's agent. The house (*below*), which is shown to the public, has for some years been in the charge of the National Trust. Cockermouth today is a busy market town and holiday resort.

STY HEAD TARN AND GREAT END

STY HEAD TARN (1,430 feet above sea-level) lies close to the junction of paths from Borrowdale to Wasdale and to Great Langdale. The pass to Wasdale, the true Sty Head, rises to 1,600 feet. Great End (2,984 feet) is so called because it forms the northern end of the Scafell *massif*. Its north face falls in a fine precipice, seamed by dark gullies; one of which (the black cleft visible just below the apparent summit) is spanned by a remarkable natural arch.

DERWENTWATER, LOOKING TOWARDS BORROWDALE

MUCH of the charm of Derwentwater lies in its subtle variety. Contrast this view with those on pages 18 and 19. Here the lower slopes, richly clothed in foliage, are overhung by the naked crags of the central group of mountains, conspicuous among which are Great End (*right*) and Glaramara (*right-centre*). At their feet the little Castle Crag, crowned by a pre-historic fortress overlooking the River Derwent, guards the entrance to Borrowdale.

39

AMID THE FELLS

SPRINKLING TARN (*left, above*) is the source of the Derwent. Great End rises to the south and Great Gable on the west; Kirkfell (2,631 feet) appears in the gap between them. The cottage (*above*) at Stonethwaite, overhung by its attendant yew, displays charming features of many Lakeland homes: the cosy whitewashed porch (with stone seats); the attractive centre-hung windows; the roof of silver-grey, weathered slates; and the dry-stone wall, which so often becomes a veritable rock-garden. The growing of coppice wood for charcoal has long been given up, but there is still a flourishing timber industry (*left, below*) in the Lake District. Pit-props, fence-posts and rails, timber for joinery and for the manufacture of bobbins for the cotton mills of Lancashire, are the principal uses to which it is put.

BASSENTHWAITE WATER AND SKIDDAW

THE RASH FIELD, RYDAL

OVERLOOKING Rydal Water is the sloping field, sometimes known as Dora's Field after the poet's daughter, which Wordsworth purchased in 1826. It was in turn the poet's grandson who in 1935 gave the field to the National Trust. Rydal Water, well seen on pages 70-1, is among the smallest of the lakes; a tiny jewel whose charm lies in the perfection of its setting.

The South

THE southern part of the Lake District is perhaps better known than any other. For one thing, it can now be easily reached in all sorts of ways, and comfortable long-distance motor-coaches have made it accessible from all parts of the country. If Keswick is to be called the hub of the North, Grasmere is the hub of the South. If Keswick is rich in literary associations, Grasmere is so too. It is interesting to recall that Wordsworth is associated with all the three Lakeland counties. He was born at Cockermouth in Cumberland, went to school at Hawkshead in Lancashire, and lived and worked and died at Grasmere in Westmorland. In this, as in all other ways, Wordsworth makes the whole of the Lake District a great unity.

The lakes themselves are perhaps the chief adornment of the South, for they are scattered about in the richest variety. There is Grasmere itself, with Loughrigg Fell and Silver How and Helm Crag about it; little Rydal Water with its tiny islets; Elterwater in Langdale, and Esthwaite Water near Hawkshead. But the chief attraction is, of course, Lake Windermere, the largest of all the lakes and possessing a distinctive life of its own. The very name of Windermere has a lovely sound like so many of the names of Lakeland, and it lives most fully up to its name. It has an incomparable setting, and viewed from any of the surrounding fells, such as Wansfell Pike or Orrest Head, it is a perfect thing of beauty. Incidentally, from these famous viewpoints there are wonderful views of Wetherlam and the Langdale Pikes.

Those who know the life of the Broads, or the life of the Thames, know the indescribable charm that attaches to the life of particular places. Lake Windermere possesses this charm in a most striking way. Newby Bridge at the foot of the lake, where the waters pass into the River Leven, presents one notable aspect of it. The stretch of the lake from Newby Bridge to Lakeside passes for the most part between comparatively narrow banks, with charming islands and landing places, and where no steamer intrudes. To laze in a boat, to fish for perch, to picnic on one of the islands and watch all the wealth of form and colour is to taste one of the peculiar joys of Windermere. From Newby Bridge, too, the famous Priory at Cartmel is well within range, as is also the beautiful Rusland Valley, lying between Windermere and Coniston. But Bowness, higher up Lake Windermere, presents a totally different kind of life. It is full of bustle and animation in the summer months, with boating and sailing and fishing in plenty.

Coniston Water is another of the more famous lakes, and John Ruskin lived on its shores at Brantwood for many years. In addition to the larger lakes like Windermere, and the smaller ones like Elterwater, there are innumerable tarns scattered everywhere. Blea Tarn, lying between Dungeon Gill and Fell Foot, was the scene of Wordsworth's *Excursion,* and it is from here that one of the most famous views of the Langdale Pikes is to be seen. For the Langdale Pikes and Coniston Old Man are two of the most famous mountains in the South. The Pikes —Harrison Stickle and the Pike o' Stickle—are perhaps the most photographed peaks in England; but they are not merely satisfying to look at, they are equally satisfying to climb. Travellers on the way to Carlisle and Scotland by train can catch ravishing glimpses of the Pikes from the railway, and there is a view of them from the Bowness Road near Ambleside, which has some claim to being one of the loveliest distant views in England.

To climb the Pikes from Dungeon Gill is one of the memorable things to do. On the way up, if the day is hot, there are still, deep, cool pools in which to bathe; and the sight of Stickle Tarn high up among the hills, with the two peaks themselves still waiting to be climbed, fills the mind with a kind of exaltation. A visit at the same time to Sergeant Man, High Raise and High White Stones gives a view of the mountains never to be forgotten. Coniston Old Man, Bowfell, Scafell Pikes, Pillar, Gable, the fells of Buttermere, Skiddaw, Blencathra, Helvellyn, and the full length of Windermere thrown in. Again the whole of the Lake District is seen to be one, and it is literally true that one is "breathless with adoration."

In this district then there are to be found the tiny hamlets, the quaint villages, the little sturdy towns, the quiet valleys, the peaceful streams, the mighty mountains, the placid lakes, and the authentic and memorable breath of true Lakeland. It is true that all these things do not appeal to everybody. Even Charles Lamb, writing to Wordsworth, could say that "separate from the pleasure of your company, I don't much care if I never see a mountain in my life." He preferred the movement and the life to be found in the Strand and Fleet Street and Covent Garden. But when Lamb did see Helvellyn he wrote in a kind of ecstasy about it. The truth is that the sight of natural beauty satisfies a very deep-seated instinct in men and women; and it is a very good and desirable thing that this lovely Lake District should be made accessible to all. I am not unaware of the fears expressed in some quarters about the dangers which attend such a policy, and I know how much country folk have suffered at the hands of some visitors from the towns. But grounds of complaint will vanish as the standards of good manners are raised and as education spreads. Mr. Belloc has reminded us that "the love of England has in it the love of landscape as has the love of no other country." It is from that love, more widely diffused than ever, that true preservation of places of natural beauty will spring.

YEW-TREE FARM, YEWDALE, CONISTON

THIS old farmstead, at the entrance to the romantic valley of Tilberthwaite, is noted for its splendid yew trees and also for its fine example of an outside spinning gallery. Such galleries are rare today, but at one time each farm had its own, where combing, carding and spinning were carried on by hand. The fleeces were home-clipped, washed and dyed.

CONISTON AND JOHN RUSKIN

WHEN seen across the lake from the Brantwood side, Lancashire's highest mountain, the Old Man (2,633 feet), appears to brood over the village of Coniston, lying at its foot (*bottom, left*). Apart from summer visitors, the chief occupation hereabouts is quarrying, the finest-quality roofing slate being taken from the Old Man and neighbouring quarries. The view northwards from the Old Man (*top, left*) takes in the long range of Helvellyn, which is continued south-eastwards by Fairfield and the Ambleside fells. Nearer are the twin-peaked Wetherlam (2,502 feet), and the hollow in which lies Levers Water. At Brantwood (*above*), on the eastern side of Coniston Water, Ruskin lived for thirty years and wrote some of his most famous essays. Before Ruskin the house was the home of three distinguished literary figures: first the poet Gerald Massey and then the Lynn-Lintons; after Ruskin, his friend William Gershom Collingwood, historian and novelist, continued the literary tradition.

TARN HOWS, NEAR CONISTON

ANN TYSON'S COTTAGE

WILLIAM WORDSWORTH started school in Hawkshead at Whitsuntide, 1778. For the eight years of his schooldays there he lodged at the cottage of Ann Tyson, and this picture shows the cottage much as it must have been in her time. Now the outside staircase has a wooden railing, and the flagged yard is an old English garden.

WORDSWORTH'S SCHOOL

THE old Grammar School at Hawkshead was founded by Archbishop Sandys in 1585, but the building seen today dates from 1675. The mullioned windows and the sundial, set aslant in the wall, are notable, and one can still see the desk (*left*) on which Wordsworth carved his initials. The excellent grounding he received enabled him to have "a full twelve months' start" of the freshmen at St. John's College, Cambridge, whither he went in 1787.

52

HAWKSHEAD AND WETHERLAM

IN ANCIENT times an important market town, Hawkshead is today the quaintest small town in the whole of Lancashire. Its crooked streets and cobbled yards and "nooks," reached under archways, with gables and penthouses at all angles, are unique. Seen here across the Priest's Pot (*see* page 55), the village is dominated by the church, seated, said Wordsworth, on her hill "like a throned lady"; and overlooked by the bold crest of the mountain Wetherlam.

WINDERMERE: THE SOUTHERN REACHES

ONE of England's finest panoramas unrolls below
those who climb Orrest Head (684 feet), close to
the station at Windermere. Whilst the northward
view commands a great array of lofty mountains,
the southward aspect is in striking contrast. Its
feature is the sinuously curving line of the lake,
stretching away between lower hills, many of
them clothed from head to foot in rich wood-
lands. Opposite Belle Isle, the largest island,
Bowness Bay opens out; beyond which a prominent "neb" on the right and a less prominent
one on the left mark the position of the ferry.
The remains of a pseudo-Grecian temple may
be seen at Storrs Point, jutting out a little way
beyond. To Storrs in 1825 came Sir Walter Scott,
Canning (shortly to become Prime Minister),
Wordsworth, "Christopher North" (Professor
John Wilson), and other notables, for a grand
water-party in honour of Scott's birthday, with
a three-hour procession of decorated boats.

54

RURAL PEACE BESIDE ESTHWAITE WATER

ESTHWAITE WATER is one of the few remaining privately owned meres. About a mile and a half in length, its greatest breadth is half a mile. Its shores have a special character which explains the name. Several rounded promontories jut out, each an island but for the narrow isthmus joining it to the shore. To these the name "ees" is given; a "thwaite" is a clearing. The name therefore means: "the island-studded water amid the clearing." Just beyond the head of the lake, a small circular pond (seen on page 53) bears the name "Priest's Pot"—at one time the vivarium of the monks from Furness Abbey, which had large estates near-by. Hawkshead, less than a mile away, was the centre of their hunting ground and timber forest, and the manor courthouse still remains. Its church was referred to as an old one in 1219; the present building dates from the fifteenth century. It contains a fine altar-tomb, dated 1578, bearing effigies of William and Margaret Sandys, and a curious old muniment chest carved out of a single tree trunk.

"SWANS" AT BOWNESS AND NEWBY BRIDGE

A MILE below its outflow from Windermere, the Leven passes beneath Newby Bridge (*above*), a fine example of the local craft in bridge building, in which solidity and grace are happily blended. Close by stands the comfortable Swan Hotel. Midway between Lakeside, at the foot, and Waterhead Pier, at the head, is Bowness Pier—busiest spot on Windermere. British Railways operate five steam- or motor-driven vessels, of which the sister ships *Swan* (*seen left*) and *Teal* are miniature liners, carrying thousands of visitors daily in the season. The sail along the full length of Windermere is a pleasant one, and the best way of seeing England's largest lake.

56

BOWNESS CHURCH AND FERRY

ON THE site of St. Martin's Church, Bowness, there has been Christian worship for more than a thousand years. The present building, dating from 1483, is notable for the fine glass in the east window, some of which—early fourteenth-century work—came probably from Cartmel Priory. On one pane appear the arms of the Washington family—the stars and stripes. The steam cable-ferry at Bowness forms a vital link in the road system of the Lake District. Maintained jointly by the county councils of Westmorland and Lancashire, it operates throughout the year, and on an average summer day transports hundreds of vehicles across the lake.

A HAMLET AMID THE FELLS

TROUTBECK, near Windermere—not to be confused with another village of the same name in Cumberland—is a hamlet of unusual charm, containing many gems of local architecture; notably Town End (National Trust), a typical Westmorland yeoman's home. Here, too, is the famous inn, "The Mortal Man." The mountains on the east form the southern end of the High Street range, along which ran the Roman Road from Brougham to Ambleside.

OLD BRIDGE HOUSE, AMBLESIDE

THIS quaint building, spanning the Stock Beck, is owned by the National Trust, and is now an antique shop. In the eighteenth century it was probably a garden house. Ambleside, a favourite centre for touring the southern Lake District, has undergone many changes, but still retains several picturesque corners. Its coaching inns were famous, and their successors today have a high reputation for comfort and food. Ambleside keeps up its Rush-bearing ceremony.

AMBLESIDE AND WANSFELL PIKE

STOCKGILL FORCE, AMBLESIDE

FOAMING through a wooded dingle, the Stock Beck makes a series of pretty cascades, of which that seen here has a fall of 70 feet, apparently sheer, though actually broken midway. The effect is heightened by the fall being double, a rock dividing the water into two streams. No one likes paying to see waterfalls; after many years of such complaints, Stockgill Force, half a mile from Ambleside, has been acquired by the local council and access is now free.

SKELWITH FORCE

JUST above the graceful Skelwith Bridge, three miles from Ambleside, the Brathay, after flowing out of Elterwater, dashes down this little waterfall. The height is only 12 feet, but enough water pours over to create an iridescent cloud of "water smoke." The power of the fall was formerly used to operate a sawmill and bobbin factory. Looking upstream, Harrison Stickle (2,403 feet), five miles distant and the higher of the Langdale Pikes, can be seen.

THE CURVE OF GREAT LANGDALE, FROM CRINKLE CRAGS

THE LANGDALES

AT THE left, one is looking up Great Langdale from the slate quarry at Thrang, with the Langdale Pikes rising straight in front to 2,400 feet. The dark shadow masks the grand precipice of Pavey Ark, below which lies, out of sight, the lovely Stickle Tarn. The tent-shaped summit is Harrison Stickle, left of which the upper part of the Dungeon Gill, celebrated in poems by Coleridge and Wordsworth, appears as a black gash. Lingmoor, the hill on the extreme left, separates Great Langdale from its neighbour, Little Langdale. To Blea Tarn (*left, below*) the Pikes form a fine background. Pike o' Stickle is the rounded summit at the extreme left; between it and Harrison Stickle appears Loft Crag, the cliffs below which are the famous "gymnasium" of Gimmer Crag, resort of the rubber-shoed rock climbers. Slaters' Bridge, in Little Langdale (*below*), is a primitive structure, very typical of the dales, spanning the infant Brathay. This view, looking towards the Wrynose Pass, which can just be seen, shows well the charm and grandeur of the Langdale scenery.

PIKE O' STICKLE, FROM LOFT CRAG

The thimble-shaped top of Pike o' Stickle (2,323 feet) forms a conspicuous landmark. The steepness of its front—an angle of forty-five degrees, continued unbroken for 2,000 feet—is exceptional. The scale can be judged by the two tiny figures on the summit. Beside the rough scree-shoot called Pike o' Stickle Gully, traces of a prehistoric stone-axe factory were recently found. On the skyline appear Great End (*left*) and the massive head of Great Gable.

ROCK CLIMBING IN LANGDALE

ROCK climbs are classified according to the following degrees of difficulty: easy, moderate, difficult, very difficult, severe and very severe. The climb illustrated, on Scout Crag, is classed as no more than "difficult"! Climbers move one at a time; the second man, tied on to the rock, safeguarding the leader until he is in turn "belayed," when the second climbs up to join him. The process is then repeated, pitch by pitch, to the top of the rock climb.

RYDAL WATER FROM LOUGHRIGG FELL

THE POET LAUREATE'S HOME

IN 1813 Wordsworth came to Rydal Mount (*above*), which remained his home until his death in 1850. Here he was visited by Emerson, De Quincey, Lockhart, Thomas and Matthew Arnold, George Eliot, Harriet Martineau and many others. (Keats called but found Wordsworth away from home.) Wordsworth succeeded Southey as Poet Laureate in 1843.

WORDSWORTH'S SEAT

WORDSWORTH is said to have spent many an hour in silent contemplation on the huge rock (*seen above*) on the shore of Rydal Water known as "Wordsworth's Seat." In his time the view over the tranquil waters of the mere was not obscured by the trees which have now grown up. But it is extremely unlikely that—as is sometimes claimed—any great amount of poetry was actually written here, for it is known that Wordsworth preferred locomotion when in the act of literary composition. He would pace up and down, muttering his verses, while the faithful Dorothy, his sister, wrote every word down carefully in a notebook, the rough draft being later polished and re-written. The set of stepping stones (*below*) crossing the Rothay not far from Rydal was often used by Wordsworth on his rambles.

HEART OF THE WORDSWORTH COUNTRY

At Grasmere one is in the very heart of the Wordsworth country. Across the lake rises Helm Crag, its summit strewn with a wild confusion of rocks. One group is known as "The Lion and the Lamb" and another as "The Old Woman Playing the Organ." In 1799 Wordsworth, with his sister Dorothy, moved into Dove Cottage (*right, above*). Hither in 1802 he brought his bride, Mary Hutchinson, and here during the next seven years some of his finest poetry was written. Every year thousands make the pilgrimage to the cottage, whose interior is kept today in a condition very similar to that of Wordsworth's time. Grasmere Church (*right, below*), dedicated to St. Oswald, has few pretensions to architectural merit, as Wordsworth freely acknowledged. "Not raised in nice proportions was the pile" was his comment on its massive barn-like structure. The Poets' Corner in the churchyard contains the graves of William and Mary Wordsworth; their daughter Dora, with her husband, Edward Quillinan; Dorothy Wordsworth; and Hartley Coleridge, son of S. T. Coleridge.

OLD CUSTOMS AT GRASMERE

GRASMERE'S Rush-bearing procession takes place on the Saturday nearest to St. Oswald's Day (5 August), and has an unbroken recorded history of more than three centuries; the ceremony goes back far earlier. Playing a traditional march tune, the village band accompanies the elected Queen, whilst children carry sprays of flowers, with ferns and rushes, often worked into traditional patterns. Grasmere sports, held every August, are world-famous. Wrestling (Cumberland and Westmorland style), hound trails and foot races arouse great excitement in the huge audience, and the climax comes with the thrilling Guides' Race.

CARTMEL—THE PRIORY GATEWAY

THE little market town of Cartmel—full of solid, stone-built houses with graceful eighteenth-century doorways—has been described as a cathedral city in miniature. Its beautiful Priory Church dates from the twelfth century, and was bought by the townspeople at the Dissolution. It is unique in having the upper storey of the tower set diagonally upon the lower portion. The fourteenth-century Gate House is now a museum and artist's studio.

STRIDING EDGE, HELVELLYN

On its eastern side, facing Ullswater, Helvellyn sends out two rocky arms enclosing the basin in which lies Red Tarn (2,356 feet), highest situated of all the mountain tarns. The northerly arm is Swirrel Edge; that to the south the famous Striding Edge, illustrated here. Its crest is a succession of shattered pinnacles the traverse of which involves some pretty scrambling, but most walkers follow a track which keeps just below the actual ridge.

The Eastern Dales

To show how these divisions of the Lake District merge into one another it is only necessary to take one of the many attractive walks from Grasmere. You can travel through the valley which runs up between Dollywaggon Pike and Fairfield, past Grisedale Tarn, and come to the charm of Ullswater at Patterdale. This links the South and the East in a morning's pleasant walking, just as that other charming walk from Grasmere through the hills to Rosthwaite in Borrowdale links the South and the North.

Ullswater runs from Patterdale to Pooley Bridge, a distance of seven miles, and it was at Patterdale that a great scholar and student of the Lake counties, W. G. Collingwood, who wrote a book of that name—*The Lake Counties*—said that here the grandest of lake scenery was to be found because the contour lines fall with "broken and cliffy impetus into the level floor of water." There are two other lakes in this portion of the district about which a word or two ought to be said—Thirlmere and Haweswater. The great cities need water, and the city of Manchester draws its water from these two lakes. They have suffered a great loss of natural beauty, and some old and well-loved places have been submerged. They have both been changed into reservoirs. The level of Thirlmere was raised some fifty feet and its area was vastly increased, and Haweswater has undergone considerable transformation. Ennerdale Water was but recently saved from a similar fate. The needs of great cities must of course be met, and the local authorities concerned are not unmindful of the need to preserve all the natural beauty we possess; but it is inevitable that the wild and unspoilt beauty of these remote places must suffer grievously. The new National Parks and Access to the Countryside Act of 1949 offers hope that in the future the beauty of the Lake District will receive the fullest consideration at the hands of the Commissioners in all the various schemes of proposed development, whatever they may be and from whatever quarter they may come.

One of the most famous and familiar views belongs to this district also, and is worthy of a word or two of comment. Photographs of Striding Edge on Helvellyn usually show it to be much more fearsome-looking that it really is, and De Quincey called it this "awful curtain of rock." Striding Edge and Swirrel Edge enclose Red Tarn beneath them and it is a place known to many people who have never been there, because of the death of a man named Charles Gough a hundred and fifty years ago who lost his life when he fell at this lonely spot. This was sad enough, but disasters of the like kind have happened in Lakeland and been speedily forgotten. But the thing that makes this particular disaster live is the devotion of a little yellow terrier called Foxey. This faithful little dog never left his master's body for three long months. Canon Rawnsley investigated the matter fully, and though some things remain in doubt, what De Quincey called "the sublime and mysterious fidelity of the dog" is established.

Even so, the matter might well have passed into forgetfulness had it not been for the fact that in the year following the disaster two great men visited the spot —Sir Walter Scott and Wordsworth. Both men were moved to write poems on the subject, and many generations of schoolboys have been compelled to learn them by heart. Scott's poem, which begins:

> *I climbed the dark brow of the mighty Helvellyn,*
> *Lakes and mountains beneath me gleamed misty and wide,*

has one quite magical touch which brings to the imagination the great solitude where the body lay, and the faithful little dog keeping its lonely vigil, in the lines:

> *How long did'st thou think that his silence was slumber—*
> *When the wind waved his garment how oft did'st thou start?*

Helvellyn and Ullswater dominate this part of the Lake District, but it is infinitely rich in lovely villages like Askham, with eighteenth-century cottages and a village green and charming inn; little churches like Wythburn, at the foot of Helvellyn; charming little lakes like Brothers Water, to be seen after going through the Kirkstone Pass; noble mountains like St. Sunday Crag; and valleys filled in the season with wild flowers of every kind.

But it is on Helvellyn and Ullswater that public attention has been chiefly centred. There is a wealth of writing on both the mountain and the lake, and in that writing is to be found the insistence on what may be called the everyday things that for the most part go unacknowledged, such as the colours and scents and sounds that belong to Lakeland at all seasons of the year. Summer is no doubt the best season of all, and for most people it is also the time of holiday. But there are special and characteristic joys in all the seasons. To see the great mountains covered with snow in the depth of winter is to discover a new and greater majesty; to see the vigour of returning life in Springtime is in a very deep sense to renew one's own life; and to revel in the glory of Autumn's colouring is to savour one of life's major pleasures. "The earth is full of wonderful things," said Grey of Fallodon, "and I like to dwell on two especially. One is the infinite beauty of the world; and the other, separate from and yet inseparably connected with the first, is the power of man to perceive the beauty and to be moved by it." The Eastern Dales nobly exemplify his theme.

LONG SLEDDALE

TYPICAL of the scenery of the eastern dales is this view of Long Sleddale. The quiet hamlet of Garnett Bridge straddles the little River Sprint which, with many a rapid and water-break, hurries to join the Kent. In former days more than one mill made use of the falls here; now the corn mill alone remains—one of the few still working locally. As "Long Whindale," the dale figures in Mrs. Humphry Ward's *Robert Elsmere*. Like the neighbouring Kentmere, it is a long, narrow trench, steep-sided and gently winding, with farmsteads scattered along the well-cultivated strath, and an upper reach which is rocky and lonely.

HEAD OF HAWESWATER

HAWESWATER was originally two and a half miles
long and, standing at a height of 694 feet, was
the highest placed of all the lakes. Now, as a
reservoir for Manchester, its pent-up waters
stretch for more than four miles, and top water
level is some 790 feet. At its southern end the
new lake sends a tongue (*shown in the picture*)
lapping up into the very heart of the fells. The
craggy front of Harter Fell (2,569 feet) is reflected
in the still waters. To its left the Gatesgarth
Pass winds over into Long Sleddale. To the
right of Harter Fell the beginning of the path
leading over to Kentmere by the Nan Bield
Pass may be seen. The long, rocky ridge, crowned
by a dry-stone wall, is appropriately named
Rough Crag, and runs up to High Street (2,718
feet). Below it, at the mouth of the wide valley
of Riggindale, the ruins of the dispossessed
farms may still be seen, pathetic reminders of
pre-reservoir days. The old hamlet of Mardale
Green, with the church, school and Dun Bull
Inn, is completely submerged by the water.

82

SWINDALE, FROM SHAP FELLS

AN ATTRACTIVE approach to the Lake District is to start from Shap. Striking westwards from its long main street, one crosses the Lowther either at Keld, with its ancient chapel (in which the first service for more than three hundred years was recently held), or close to the venerable ruin of Shap Abbey. From either place a wandering track leads past the lonely farmsteads of Ralfland Forest until, on rounding a moorland spur, the ground drops below one's feet and the sequestered valley of Swindale is suddenly revealed. The camera, with its simultaneous equation of foreground and background, is unable to portray the authentic impression—of flat-bottomed valley inurned in steep fells—but, to the living eye, Swindale is one of the most characteristic of all Lakeland dales. Its head has real grandeur. In the course of time Swindale may, alas, join Mardale as a supplier of water for thirsty Manchester. Over the low ridge on the right runs the old pony-track to Mardale, which lies just beyond the first ridge, overlooked by the sharp peak of Kidsty Pike (2,560 feet).

ANGLERS AT HAYESWATER GILL

THE picture shows the Hayeswater Gill, which flows from the large, finely-shaped tarn of that name, just below its junction with the Pasture Beck. Grey Crag (2,286 feet) forms the background. The mountain becks abound in trout, although these are generally small. This is to be expected; sizable fish depend on an ample food supply, and a sudden spate will wash away all the food which has formed on the rocks. Even so, sport is often good.

THE VALE OF LOWTHER

LOWTHER CASTLE (*above*) and the village of Askham (*below*) stand on opposite sides of the Lowther a few miles above its junction with the Eamont, flowing out of Ullswater. The castle, former seat of the Earls of Lonsdale, is surrounded by a stately park of huge extent, and was one of the great mansions of England. Of no great age, the name which it was sometimes given—"The Windsor of the North"—hence seemed scarcely appropriate. Its most imposing feature is the castellated north front, 420 feet long. Once it contained a fine collection of paintings; now its appearance is somewhat forlorn. Askham, a cluster of sturdy cottages and inns grouped around the village green with the ancient Askham Hall standing close by, is among the most attractive of Westmorland hamlets.

LOVELY ULLSWATER

MANY regard Ullswater, second in size of the English lakes, as the first in beauty. Certainly in its combination of softness with grandeur it is not easily rivalled. It has three well-marked reaches. The lowest is pastoral in character, whilst the middle reach is overhung by a line of steep fells on its southern shore, opposite which rise the glorious wooded and park-like slopes of Gowbarrow Fell and Glencoyne Park. The view at the left is taken from the latter. The glens which open on the south side of the middle reach lead into the wild recesses of the High Street range, where is the sanctuary of the last herd of wild red deer now left in England. Gowbarrow Hall (*below*) is a typical sheep farm. The photograph shows sheep at shearing time driven out into a meadow so that the sun can dry the wool, damped by a heavy shower, before the animals go to the shearer. The highest reach of Ullswater is the grandest; the head of the lake (*left, below*) forms a scene of solemn impressiveness. St. Sunday Crag (2,756 feet) is the dominant fell; to its right rocky ridges lead up towards the top of Helvellyn.

HELVELLYN

HELVELLYN (3,118 feet) is the highest point of a long range of hills extending for nearly nine miles. From the summit the view eastwards embraces Ullswater, backed by the fells of the High Street range, with the giants of the high Pennines in the far distance. To the west can be seen most of the chief mountains of the Lake District—from the Coniston group in the south-west by way of the Scafells, Great Gable, Pillar, the Buttermere fells and the Grasmoor group round to Skiddaw and Blencathra in the north. Most dramatic are the crags falling steeply to the Red Tarn, girdled by the two grim Edges and reflecting the cone of Catchedicam. The upper picture shows the summit (2,832 feet) of the great limb which is joined to Helvellyn by Striding Edge, most of whose rock towers are obscured by it. In the centre stands Helvellyn itself, its cliffs crowned by a snow-cornice. The lower picture shows Helvellyn's summit, seen from the track over the highest slopes of the mountain. The dark object is the shelter, a mere cross of walls. The photograph shows the great hollows, locally called "coves," scooped out of the ridge on its cold, east side by the glaciers.

THE KIRKSTONE PASS

HERE we are looking down the pass towards Brothers Water (seen at the foot of the wooded slope) and Patterdale. The steep screes of Caudale Moor sweep down to the road; beyond them Place Fell (2,154 feet) forms a solid background. Kirkstone Pass is said to derive its name from a conspicuous pointed rock, shaped roughly like a church; but this may be only half the truth, for it seems certain that, in the dark days of persecution, the Covenanters used to meet in this remote spot where they could worship in freedom.

THIRLMERE AND HELVELLYN

THIRLMERE, in former times called Leathes Water, was originally shaped somewhat like a swan, and was crossed at its narrowest part by a quaint wooden bridge on stone piers. Since its acquisition by Manchester Corporation for a reservoir, the level has been twice raised and it is now four miles long, with steep, regular sides. Here we are looking from the road on the west side across the water to Browncove Crags (2,819 feet) on Helvellyn.

PATTERDALE AND BROTHERS WATER

PATTERDALE is said to take its name from St. Patrick, and the saint's well may still be seen. The village (*below*) is an excellent centre for exploring the beautiful surroundings of Ullswater, and the three romantic glens—Grisedale, Deepdale and Dovedale (the last shown on page 95)—which penetrate deep into the fells on the dale's western side. The view up Patterdale itself (*left, below*) shows the rich alluvial land of the valley bottom, and the hanging woods which clothe the slopes below Lingy Crag. The rounded fell is Hartsop Dodd, and the semi-circle of steep crags beyond it encloses the hanging valley of Caudale. To the left of Hartsop Dodd is seen the valley of the Pasture Beck, running up into Threshthwaite Cove, the depression between Caudale Moor (2,502 feet) and High Street. Brothers Water (*left*) is among the smallest of the lakes. Standing at its head is the bluff High Hartsop Dodd, with a fine amphitheatre of crags running round to Dove Crag; Hartsop Hall is seen in the trees below.

HARTSOP AND DOVEDALE

BETWEEN the head of Ullswater and the foot of the Kirkstone Pass lies Hartsop, a place of many old cottages, several with outside galleries and staircases. At the left (*top*) we are looking down the green strath of Patterdale to the head of the lake, with Place Fell looming on the right. Above is seen the old farmhouse of Hartsop Hall, standing in the splendid valley of Dovedale and overlooked by the great cliffs of Dove Crag (2,605 feet). Farther right is Hart Crag (2,698 feet). The Patterdale Foxhounds often meet at Hartsop, whence they are seen (*below*, *left*) setting out over the old packhorse bridge. Historic runs have been made by this famous pack, which hunts the rough country about the crags of Fairfield and Helvellyn, the fells of the High Street range and those around Kirkstone Pass.

WESTWARD FROM FLEETWITH PIKE

IT IS not really a valley of three lakes that one sees from Fleetwith Pike, for Loweswater lies in a lateral valley of its own. Ages ago, indeed, it was a valley of *one* lake; the delta built up by the Sail Beck (page 99) has gradually pushed its way across to divide one lake into two—Buttermere the upper one (nearest the camera) and Crummock the lower. The bulky Melbreak overlooks the latter; behind it rise the little-visited Lamplugh Fells.

The Western Dales

THIS particular section of the Lake District, although it comes last in the book, is a very special favourite with the discerning. In all the vast literature of Lakeland there is to be observed a very intimate and loving note when the writers speak of this area. Its chief claim to fame is that it has been, and still is, the home of the true climbers and the lovers of solitary places. It is not too much to say that the names of Wasdale and Wastwater conjure up, for the discerning folk of whom we speak, the true glories of the Lake District. The lake itself is nearly three miles long and is some 200 feet above sea-level. But it is the marvellous setting of the lake which gives it its austerity and grandeur. On one side the famous Screes rise to a height of nearly 2,000 feet and to the north-west lie Middlefell and Seatallan and Yewbarrow, with Red Pike and Steeple behind, and the exquisitely beautiful tarns at their feet. Running north-west from the head of Wastwater is the valley known as Mosedale, with the famous Black Sail Pass between Yewbarrow and Kirkfell, whilst to the north-east runs the valley of Lingmell Beck up to Styhead Pass between Great Gable and Lingmell.

At Wasdale Head is the tiny ancient church, and the celebrated Wasdale Head Hotel, which may be said in the local phrase to be miles from anywhere, certainly thirteen miles from Seascale on the coast. Famous climbers from all parts of the country have gathered here from time to time, and there used to be kept at the hotel a most valuable book in which celebrated climbers recorded their first ascents of new climbs for the guidance of all who should come after. It was said that this book could only be seen by those who had shown themselves to be worthy of reading it by being climbers in the full sense of that word and members of the great brotherhood.

In days past the hotel had for its landlord Will Ritson, a great wrestler and a great wit, and a great "character." Many of his dialect sayings are preserved and repeated, and one of the folk-sayings that have come down from his day, making reference to his habit of humorous exaggeration, is that Wasdale has the highest mountain, the deepest lake, the smallest church and the biggest liar in all England. Of Ennerdale Water I have already spoken, and the Pillar Rock is the magnet for climbers in this area.

It is a great change from Ennerdale and Wasdale to pass to the peace and quiet of Buttermere and the charms of Crummock Water and Loweswater. All three lakes may be seen in their beauty from Honister, set in their surrounding hills. Two other notable places in this part of the Lake District must just receive mention—Eskdale and the Duddon Valley. Eskdale belongs to Cumberland, and is a vale of surpassing beauty and fascination. Immense crags of rock rise above charming woods, and all along the vale are little collections of houses. Near to Eskdale are two characteristic features of Lakeland in Birker Force and Dalegarth Force, both lovely waterfalls, which after rain present the most astonishing sight, Dalegarth Force falling over 60 feet of rock into the most delightful ravine. Hereabouts, too, is the tiny Devoke Water, some 800 feet above the sea. The Duddon Valley is famous for itself, but it has been made more famous still by the fact of Wordsworth's Sonnets.

I may perhaps end these rather disjointed Introductions by saying that the Lake District is much more than any description can convey, and much more than any photograph can portray. There is a *spirit* of Lakeland only to be gained by those who go there and imbibe it for themselves. Age makes no difference, for Lakeland has something for everybody. In boyhood and youth, in the full strength of manhood or womanhood, in middle age, and in old age, the spell of this land never fails. Wordsworth was a middle-aged man when the famous Duddon Sonnets were at last published. For nearly fifty years he had imbibed that spirit of which I have spoken. His really active life was over, but he could leave to all who follow those lovely lines:

> *For, backward, Duddon, as I cast my eyes*
> *I see what was, and is, and will abide:*
> *Still glides the stream and shall for ever glide,*
> *The Form remains, the Function never dies;*
> *While we, the brave, the mighty, and the wise,*
> *We Men, who in our morn of youth defied*
> *The elements, must vanish: be it so!*
> *Enough if something from our hands have power*
> *To live, and act, and serve the future hour;*
> *And if, as toward the silent tomb we go,*
> *Through love, through hope, and faith's transcendent dower*
> *We feel that we are greater than we know.*

By the time this book appears the Lake District will be a National Park. In the fullest sense it will be a national possession for all time. The preservation of its beauty in the larger sense is in the hands of the specially appointed Commissioners, and on their wisdom and foresight the future of the Lake District depends. But it should be a matter of honour to every visitor to regard this place as a great sanctuary, and to safeguard it in every way; for in the voluntary observance of a true code of behaviour by those for whom the National Park has been created lies the surest hope of an unspoilt land.

AMID THE GRASMOOR FELLS

WALKERS from Buttermere to Keswick can take a path running on either side of the Sail
Beck. It is one of the quietest walks in the district, overhung by the steep screes of Wandhope, Eel Crags and Sail. After crossing the head of the pass at nearly 1,600 feet, the
valley of the Rigg Beck leads down into lower Newlands.

FLEETWITH PIKE REFLECTED IN BUTTERMERE

LOOKING DOWN LOWESWATER

IT IS a rule that to gain the finest impression of
any lake one should look upwards from the foot,
so that the mountains normally grouped round
its head will make their full effect. Loweswater
is an exception. The fells at its upper end are
low and grassy, but looking downwards from
the head the subtle grouping of the mountains
which surround Crummock Water and Buttermere makes a striking picture. At the extreme
left the slope of Grasmoor (2,791 feet) runs out
of the photograph. Farther right appears the
peak of Whiteless Pike, with the narrow ridge
running up to Wandhope on its left. Behind
rises Robinson (2,417 feet), below which is the
level top of Buttermere Moss, with the little
Rannerdale Knotts in front. Crummock Water
lies, unseen, at its foot. Farther right, beyond the
sheer precipice of Honister Crag, all else is
blotted out by the enormous bulk of Melbreak
which, although only 1,676 feet, is a most
impressive hill, steep on all sides. Loweswater
is a mile long and a quarter of a mile wide.

CRUMMOCK WATER AND RED PIKE

MUCH the same size as Ennerdale and Wastwater, Crummock Water has a more varied
shoreline than either of its famous rivals among
the western lakes. This view, taken where the
road runs at the foot of the massive red flanks
of Grasmoor, looks into the peaceful nook of
Rannerdale, where the fells draw back to allow
room for a few green meadows between them
and the lake. Just beyond these the road passes
round the rocky Hause Point, where it runs on
a shelf above the water, shortly to reach Buttermere village. On the western shore the screes of
Melbreak (*right*) sweep down to the water, to
end in the little peninsula called Ling Crag,
beyond which the valley of the Scale Beck
separates Melbreak from the long range of the
Buttermere fells. The skyline reads (*right to left*)
Starling Dodd (2,085 feet), Red Pike (2,479 feet),
and High Stile (2,643 feet). The view from Red
Pike is striking. Close at hand rises the Grasmoor
group, with Skiddaw and Blencathra to its
north-east, while, to the south, the great crags
of Pillar and Steeple plunge into Ennerdale.
In addition the sea is in view, and five lakes.

SCALE FORCE, CRUMMOCK WATER

EASILY reached from Buttermere village, Scale Force, with a fall of 130 feet, is the highest in the district. (Birker Force in Eskdale, considerably higher, is more a cascade than a true waterfall.) Scale Force owes much of its impressiveness to its fine situation and to the wonderful variety of rock plants and ferns draping the rocks. Best seen after heavy rain, it is no less beautiful with only a moderate volume of water coming down.

THE QUEEN OF THE WESTERN LAKES

THE least visited of the great lakes, Ennerdale Water is one of the few places where true peace and solitude can be found. Viewed from the foot, the almost circular lower basin forms a glorious foreground to the two steep crags, Bowness Knott and Angling Crag, between which the upper reach of the lake extends, solemn and regular with, seemingly at its head, the imperious skyline of the Pillar (2,927 feet), Scoatfell and the Steeple.

LOOKING SEAWARD DOWN ENNERDALE, FROM GREEN GABLE

MAJESTIC WASTWATER

THE prevailing impression of Wastwater is one of solemn grandeur. Its regular shape and the closeness with which the surrounding fells hem it in seem to account for this effect, which is, for some, overpowering. Running almost the entire length of the south-eastern shore are the famous Screes (*below*), an impressive series of beetling crags and deep-cleft gullies, spreading out into broad fans of multi-coloured screes. The walk along the crest of Screes Mountain (1,983 feet) discloses thrilling views down the gullies to the dark surface of the lake below. There is a track along the foot of the Screes also, a little way above water level, but it is an extremely rough scramble over boulders of all sizes. At the head of the lake the perfect symmetry of the mountains is striking. On the left, Yewbarrow largely masks Kirkfell; in the centre, Great Gable fills the eye, the beautiful upstanding crags of the Napes Ridges (*well seen left, below*) forming a coronet; farther right, Lingmell (2,649 feet) slopes up to the higher Scafell Pike.

WASDALE HEAD, FROM GREAT GABLE

FROM the rocks of Great Gable, Wastwater creates a vastly different impression from that gained by looking up the lake. The steep rampart of the Screes is well displayed, as are the imposing slopes (*right*) of Yewbarrow and Buckbarrow. Beyond, the flat country of Nether Wasdale stretches away towards the sea. The tiny scattered hamlet of Wasdale Head, and the pattern of stone walls snaking over the dale bottom, are 2,000 feet below the camera.

GREAT GABLE, THE NAPES NEEDLE

THIS striking monolith, just over 100 feet high, is a popular, although difficult, climb. The top block is detached, and a climber seated upon it can cause it to rock perceptibly. The usual route up is by the large crack which runs diagonally across its lower part and then up the right-hand skyline. The roped party seen on the left of the picture is engaged on the first pitch of the Needle Ridge climb, an airy and exciting ascent of nearly 400 feet.

MUNCASTER CASTLE

THIS historic old pele tower has been since the thirteenth century the seat of the Penningtons. Built on a steep hillside overlooking Ravenglass harbour, its situation is a fine one. The magnificent view of the mountains surrounding Eskdale, seen from the terrace, is widely renowned. A treasured possession is the "Luck of Muncaster," a bowl of green glass given to the family by Henry VI, who sought refuge here after the Battle of Hexham in 1464.

ESKDALE RAILWAY AT DALEGARTH

VISITORS to Eskdale—of all ages—enjoy the beautiful trip up the charming dales of Mite and Esk which takes one from Ravenglass into the heart of Eskdale, a run of seven miles. First opened in 1875 as a mineral line, the Ravenglass and Eskdale Railway has since been converted to 15-inch gauge. The passenger coaches are open, giving uninterrupted views. Scale-model locomotives add, for the younger travellers at least, a final touch of delight.

MISTS ON THE SCAFELL RANGE, FROM UPPER ESKDALE

SCAFELL PINNACLE

THE north face of Scafell is the most impressive precipice in the Lake District. The crags are more than 600 feet high, and many difficult climbs have been worked out upon them. As a climbing ground it is only rivalled by the Pillar Rock and Dow Crag. The Pinnacle, a slender buttress springing skywards between Deep Gill and Steep Gill, offers some of the most taxing face-climbs in Britain. The face of the Pinnacle is stepped back, the actual summit being called the High Man and the "tread" of the step the Low Man. These two features are clearly shown in the photograph above, a beautiful study taken in the early morning, with the thin brightness of the sun picking out the crest of the High Man and the summit of Great Gable beyond it, whilst a long line of fleecy cloud drifts below the summits of the Grasmoor fells, nearly ten miles away.

116

DEEP GILL, SCAFELL

IN THE upper photograph one is looking down the cleft of Deep Gill, with the Pinnacle on the right (showing the Low Man), Deep Gill Buttress seeming to overhang on the left. Strangely enough the upper part of Deep Gill is no more than a rough scramble on scree, all the difficulties being confined to the lowest two pitches. The "West Wall Traverse" is a means of avoiding these difficulties, and thus gives a sporting and impressive route for non-climbers from the foot of the Scafell crags to the summit of the mountain. From the lower part of Deep Gill, Jones and Collier's climb (*right*) leads to the summit of the Low Man. It is classed as difficult, but the non-climber would consider this a gross understatement. The leader, safely belayed on a stance, is seen taking in the rope as the second man climbs up to join him.

117

THE TRACK TO SCAFELL PIKE

WHEN staying in Wasdale, a popular walk is the ascent of Scafell Pike (3,210 feet) by Brown Tongue. The picture shows the track zigzagging towards Pikes Crag, short of which the usual route swings left to gain the neck between Lingmell and the Pike, before turning up to the summit of the latter. Or, alternatively, one may branch right and proceed over Hollowstones to the Mickledore ridge—joining Scafell (*right*) with the Pike—which is seen on the skyline.

BOOT VILLAGE AND SCAFELL

THIS lovely peep into mid-Eskdale is from a point just above Dalegarth Force, which pours down its rocky gorge in the trees to the right. Slight Side, the southern shoulder of Scafell, is just out of the picture, as is the actual summit (3,162 feet), which lies back beyond the apparent crest. Looming dark on the skyline are Great Gable and the twin-peaked Kirkfell. Over the low saddle runs the pony track to Wasdale Head by Burnmoor.

FLANKS OF ESKDALE

THE rugged hills flanking mid-Eskdale are of a pink granite, stubborn and prickly, covered by a luxuriant growth of heather and bracken. Much of the tableland above is, however, excellent pasture, and the sturdy Herdwick sheep live out throughout the year, working gradually downhill of their own accord with the approach of severe weather. Mustering is confined to those occasions when the flock is to be counted, dipped, or shorn, or when, it may be, some are required for market. The cross-bred dogs, usually sporting a cast in one eye, are remarkable both for tirelessness and sagacity. The latter quality seems to be bred in the bone, for a puppy will often show great aptitude on its first outing with sheep. Dalegarth Force, although only 60 feet in height, is well worth seeing for the beauty of its situation alone. It is only a short walk from the railway station at Boot hamlet.

UPPER ESKDALE

At Brotherilkeld, the highest farm (*seen below*), begins the grandest and wildest reach of Eskdale. Indeed, the five miles from the farm to Esk Hause are probably the grandest, as they are certainly the loneliest, in Britain. There are two main tracks. One, which in the picture can be seen winding up the hill, runs along the high shelf between the Esk and the Scafell range; the other keeps close beside the stream and traverses the splendid Esk Gorge above Throstle Garth. Here there are a number of fine cascades, both on the Esk and on the Lingcove Beck, one of which is illustrated on the right. Still higher up is the impressive waterfall called Cam Spout, on the mountain stream beside which is a track leading up to Mickledore ridge. Thence Scafell Pike is easily gained, but to reach Scafell direct involves climbing the awkward little eight-foot wall of Broad Stand.

THE ESK—FROM SOURCE TO SEA

THIS fine view gives a characteristic glimpse into the higher reaches of Eskdale. Directly below is the upper part of the famous Esk Gorge, whilst beyond an intervening ridge rears up England's highest mountain, Scafell Pike (3,210 feet), crowned by a war memorial cairn to men of the Lake District. Ill Crag (3,040 feet) rises on the right. Ravenglass (*right*), a wide, lost harbour near the mouth of the Esk, is one of the oldest ports in Britain. The Romans built a fort (Clanoventa) here, and the remains of the bath house may still be seen. Not far away, on the sand dunes at Drigg Point, is a noted gullery.

SPORT IN WEST CUMBERLAND

THERE are two chief characteristics of the Cumberland and Westmorland style of wrestling. Firstly, the "hold" is a deliberate one, without preliminary sparring for position, each wrestler clasping his own hands behind his opponent's back. Secondly, a "throw" is completed when any part of a wrestler's body (other than his feet, of course) touches the ground. There is hence no "ground play." At sports meetings the wrestlers are usually dressed in white singlets and tights, with black shorts and stockings; and frequently a special prize is awarded to the wrestler who is most smartly turned out, irrespective of his success or failure in the contest. The West Cumbrian is a great lover of sports, of which the hound trail is probably the most popular, a deal of money often hanging on the result.

WORDSWORTH'S DUDDON

THE Duddon valley, celebrated by Wordsworth in a sequence of no fewer than thirty-four sonnets, would surely have become famous for its beauty had Wordsworth never written. The broad reach (*above*) which extends southwards from Cockley Beck is overlooked by strange castle-like rocks outcropping from Harter Fell. To the north, Red How largely obscures Crinkle Crags, over whose flank peers the peak of Bowfell. Lower down, below Ulpha, the Duddon, shaded by trees, glides swiftly over shingle bars from pool to pool.

RIVER DUDDON, BIRKS BRIDGE

WHERE the dale is narrowed by spurs sent down from the hills, the Duddon has carved its way through the rock barriers and foams grandly down rapids. Birks Bridge stands just below one such cascade; the sudden still pool beneath it—called a "dub"—is typical. In flood, the stream rises so rapidly that the bridge has often been completely submerged. The apertures in its walls have been left to allow easier passage for the flood waters.

COCKLEY BECK, DUDDON VALLEY

AT THE very head of the Duddon valley, in Wrynose Bottom, stands the National Trust farmhouse of Cockley Beck. Here the Roman road linking Eskdale to Langdale over the Hardknott and Wrynose passes meets the road which has ascended the valley from Duddon Bridge, whilst, northwards, a rough track runs up Mosedale, from the head of which are superb views of the Scafell range and of the great horseshoe sweeping round to Bowfell.

INDEX TO PHOTOGRAPHS

ACKNOWLEDGEMENT

The Editor is indebted to British Railways for permission to reproduce the pictures appearing on pages 54–5 (*top*), page 56 (*foot*), and page 69.

First published 1951. *Reprinted July,* 1956; *July,* 1959; *August,* 1961.
Made and printed in Great Britain by Odhams (Watford) Ltd., Watford
Copyright T.861.R3.N.